nº 419567

Manifest
Your
Best Life!

by
Dr. Roberto Jimenez

From the Author

Welcome, everyone!

My name is **Dr. Roberto Jimenez**. I am a **Psychotherapist** with **more than *20 years of clinical experience*** treating children and adults. I am a qualified MFT supervisor with over 20 years of clinical experience, and my approach to clients is eclectic, tailored to their unique needs, and wants. I work with individuals, couples, families, children, teenagers, the elderly, and LGBTQ. Manifest Your Best Life is a quick, easy-to-follow book helping individuals understand the manifestation process, from reviewing our thoughts, feelings, beliefs, and work ethics to bringing our dreams into reality. It's time to manifest your best life!

I am licensed in the following places:
- Licensed Marriage & Family Therapist in FL (MT1984)
- Licensed Mental Health Counselor in FL (MH10038)
- Independent Marriage & Family Therapist in Ohio - IMFT (F.2200249)
- Licensed Professional Counselor – LPC in Puerto Rico (4568)
- Licensed Marriage & Family Therapist - LMFT in North Carolina (2390)
- Licensed Marriage & Family Therapist - LMFT in Arkansas - (M2210004)
- Licensed Professional Counselor - LPC in Arkansas (P2210018)
- Licensed Marriage & Family Therapist - LMFT in California (Passed, pending activation)
- Licensed Marriage & Family Therapist - LMFT in New Jersey (Passed, pending activation)
- Licensed Marriage & Family Therapist - LMFT in Guam (MFT-027)
- Marriage & Family Therapist - LMFT in Minnesota (Taking the Legal and Ethics Exam in 2023)

Manifest Your Best Life!

All people have goals and dreams they aspire to achieve. However, while some attain them with confidence and ease, others barely pave their way to success through struggle. The reason for this striking difference lies in diverse mindsets these two categories of people demonstrate. While individuals, who lack belief that they can become successful, concentrate on barriers, people with high self-esteem focus on opportunities, realizing that they have all resources and competencies to actualize their boldest goals.

Mindset is something people should never underestimate. It is a mental attitude to self, others, and life in general, which defines the approach that humans use when dealing with various tasks. In the long-term perspective, it is a mindset that shapes behaviors and decisions of a person. Mindset is directly related to the outcomes people get. The most successful leaders know how to utilize the capacity of their powerful mindsets to the fullest extent when addressing complexities. They are perfectly aware of the power of manifesting, which is a phenomenon that helps convert goals and ideas into reality. It is a determination of people to stay in charge of their lives. **Manifesting encourages them to understand that they are not the victims of the circumstances.** Instead, it promotes the idea that every human shapes their destiny. **It is always important to remember that every person has all it takes to start manifesting. The key is to look into one's inner self and explore one's potential. The most crucial step for people, who want to manifest their goals and dreams into reality, is working with their mindset.**

Manifest Your Best Life!

A growth mindset is a foundation of manifesting because it is based on the idea that people can develop their abilities and skills throughout their lives. It means that all humans can upgrade themselves to the level that would allow them to achieve their goals and dreams much easier. Those with a growth mindset know that dedication and hard work will always pay off because these efforts will help them move to the next level. This mental disposition is ultimately important because it encourages people to believe that their efforts are worthwhile. It is also essential to remember that a growth mindset is something that makes people more independent. By believing that they can develop their abilities and skills, they acknowledge that a substantial part of their success depends on the quality of this work. While it is always important to seek support from others, people have to recognize that to facilitate their personal growth, they have to invest a lot of their own time and effort. By harnessing their growth mindset, humans believe that the next level of development is always attainable. This mentality drives their motivation to work more because they know that self-upgrade will bring them closer to their cherished dreams. Therefore, a growth mindset communicates the idea that people have to seek opportunities for growth inside of themselves first.

Abundance Mindset

Human mindset incorporates many different dimensions, and one of the most essential aspects of mentality that help people attain success easier is represented by focusing on abundance. Manifesting goals and dreams is a process that concentrates on the idea that the world has an unlimited amount of resources. However, many individuals have a completely different perspective, having a scarcity mindset (Davis, 2023). Instead of exploring endless opportunities the world offers, they are stuck on the belief that they do not have enough certain resources. For instance, some might think that the lack of money is their key barrier to success. Others are fixated on the idea that they do not have enough support to attain their goals. A scarcity mindset makes them feel that there will always be a shortage of resources that are crucial to their development. Indeed, this belief is often deeply rooted in negative experiences people faced earlier in life. For example, some of them were raised in a dysfunctional family, getting little to no support from their parents. Many people were born into poverty, and this fact makes them focus on scarcity forever. However, it is important to remember that the world can provide enough resources to everyone. Past or present struggles should not make people think that there will lack something forever. Life is all about change and development, and therefore, it is always crucial to cultivate an abundance mindset. The idea of abundance ultimately changes the focus of humans. Those with a scarcity mindset often choose not to move forward, fearing that they do not have enough money or support. As a result, they sabotage their success, failing to move and implement any effort at all.

Abundance mindset makes people behave in a completely different manner. It shapes their confidence that the world will offer the most relevant resources, which will support their further growth. By believing that there will always be enough of something, people are not scared to make bold changes. Abundance mindset drives their courage to fulfill their ambitions because they know that the world is full of opportunities. Therefore, it is always important to choose abundance over scarcity, remembering that the world has plenty of resources that can benefit humans.

Dr. Roberto Jimenez • *Manifest Your Best Life!*

Mindfulness

Manifesting goals and dreams is a process that requires people to develop their mindfulness. This term stands for human awareness of reality (Davis, 2023). When they clearly understand who they are, how their experiences influenced them, and what circumstances shape their current life, they can understand how to use these aspects to become better versions of themselves. Mindfulness is all about deep awareness, which helps people to accept themselves first and then identify the areas they would like to change. For example, a person, who was raised in an abusive family, should recognize how those childhood experiences influenced their current mentality. It is always important to acknowledge the impact of such traumatizing factors because they often contribute to the formation of negative thoughts about the world. Mindfulness helps people understand that since their fears might be a product of their adverse experiences, they do not necessarily reflect the actual state of things. By understanding the influence of their past, they can work with it to shape a better present. Similarly, people have to acknowledge their current circumstances, understanding how to use them for their own benefit.

Mindfulness also encourages them to explore their personalities at a deeper level. By analyzing the traits that define their approach to work, people can understand how to make this process better. For instance, if they identify that extraversion is their key personality trait, they will realize communication and networking will help them attain success. Those with lower scores of extraversion can understand that the key drivers of their development might be solitude and introspection. Accordingly, mindfulness encourages people to understand themselves better and decide whether they can harness certain aspects of their life or whether they have to address them to achieve success. This mindset allows them to convert their weaknesses and challenges into sources for growth and development. Mindfulness is essential because it helps people utilize their individual background when seeking new opportunities in life.

Optimistic Attitude

Another aspect of mindset that is exceptionally important to all individuals, who aspire to attain their goals and dreams more smoothly, is represented by an optimistic attitude. It stands for the tendency to focus on positive things in life (Davis, 2023). Still, it is important to remember that an optimistic attitude is not about disregarding the negative things entirely and living in a blissful ignorance that some factors significantly affect the quality of their wellbeing. It is hard to deny that all people face challenges at some point. However, those with a positive mindset choose not to see them as barriers to their future success. An optimistic attitude is a deliberate decision to treat even these challenges as a source of personal development. For instance, they realize that every failure makes them better, helping them learn new things and acquire skills they have never mastered before. By focusing on positive aspects of every experience they face in their lives, people can attain their goals faster because they understand that every step makes them closer to success. Therefore, gratitude is one of the most crucial components of a positive mindset because it encourages people to value all things that happen. Whenever they face obstacles, they have to change their approach and dedicate as many efforts as needed to overcome them.

Accordingly, it is essential to remember that an optimistic attitude is a powerful source of resilience. This concept refers to the ability of people to adapt to difficult situations and thrive regardless of setbacks or failures. A positive mindset is ultimately valuable because it drives their determination to get up and keep going no matter how many times they fell. One more aspect of an optimistic attitude is represented by a future-focused positive thinking. Humans have to cultivate it to manifest their goals and dreams more effectively. Indeed, if people believe that their aims are attainable, they will be more motivated to find a way to fulfill them. However, the lack of future-focused positive thinking makes the same targets look very complex and distant. As a result, a failure to integrate a positive mindset decreases motivation to work towards these goals and dreams, which seem barely attainable. Those who lack by a future-focused positive thinking constantly sabotage their success by lingering and thus ignoring the best opportunities that life offers.

Practical Exercises

The art of manifesting goals and dreams can take different forms. While some people prefer working with their current self-images, others try to imagine their future selves. Even though there is a wide range of approaches to manifesting, all of them have the same focus, encouraging people to work with their mentality and empower themselves. Every person chooses their unique path when making manifesting a part of their daily habits.

The following chapters will describe various exercises that provide practical tips on how to start manifesting and move towards one's goals.

                    Dr. Roberto Jimenez • *Manifest Your Best Life!*

Positive Affirmations

Many people struggle with developing a growth mindset, focusing on abundance, and acquiring an optimistic attitude. It happens because they were raised in an environment that affected their positive thinking. As a result, they often suffer from negative thoughts, which prevent them from implementing their goals and fulfilling their dreams. It is ultimately important to replace these limiting beliefs (Zapata, 2022). Practicing positive affirmations is one of the best solutions to this issue.

Positive affirmations are statements that promote optimistic thoughts, empowering people to think of themselves, others, and the world around them better. For instance, affirmations like "I live in a world that is full of kindness" encourage individuals to believe that they will always find empathy and support. By stating, "There is always a better tomorrow," humans concentrate on the idea that their life will improve day by day. Other positive affirmations encourage people to reframe their self-image. For instance, they can motivate themselves by saying words like "I am powerful" and "I am confident." Such positive statements help increase self-esteem and shape determination to work towards success, often working as self-fulfilling prophecies. "All I need is within me" and "I am enough" are affirmations that promote self-worth, helping people stay feel that they can create their own happiness. By creating a mental image of success, people make their brain activate areas that are responsible for actually experiencing such situations (Raypole, 2020).

There is a wide range of different affirmations, and it is ultimately important to choose or create statements that resonate with inner needs of a person. The first step is to identify the gaps and weaknesses that have to be addressed. After this, it is essential to come up with phrases that empower a person to eliminate these issues from their life. When the affirmations are chosen, it is crucial to integrate them in one's routine. For instance, a person who wants to manifest their goals and dreams should repeat each affirmation about ten times. It is better to choose a couple of the most powerful statements and concentrate on them. Usually, practice affirmations 3 to 5 minutes at least twice a day (Raypole, 2020).

The majority of people make it their habit, saying affirmations in the morning as soon as they wake up and in the night before getting into bed. Accordingly, they constantly remind themselves about the value of positive thinking. While some disbelievers say that positive affirmations do not work, they should remember that the key to success is consistency. It is better not to skip days because as soon as people become disconnected from positive affirmations, negative thoughts that have been formed for decades start devouring their mind. As a result, it is easy to lose concentration on one's success. Therefore, everyone who decides to recite positive affirmations to manifest their goals and dreams more effectively should stay patient, remembering that cognitive restructuring takes some time and effort.

1.

2.

3.

4.

5.

Dr. Roberto Jimenez • *Manifest Your Best Life!*

Vision Boards

Goal attainment is a process that ultimately depends on the ability of people to focus on things they want to get in life. At times, humans lose track of their goals, becoming disconnected from them. **Making vision boards is of the best solutions that can help people stay focused on their goals.** To create a board, they should identify what matters most. This process usually involves deep self-reflection. For example, while some women want to build a successful career, others aspire to start a happy family and become mothers. Material dreams are likely to be different as well. While people want to get the latest version of a smartphone, others desire to get a large mansion.

The most important step in the self-reflection process is to *identify goals that are relevant to a person at the given moment.* Those who want to make vision boards should also analyze whether their goals actually reflect their desires. Indeed, it often happens that people want something solely because they are influenced by the desires of others. When some things are considered valuable in society, it might be hard to withstand the pressure. Therefore, people have to make sure that they choose goals that genuinely reflect their individual aspirations and unique values. Next, they can proceed with the creation of the visual board itself. There are many sources of visuals that range from old magazines to the websites like Pinterest. The key point in this process is to choose visual representations that illustrate the chosen goals as accurately as possible. After getting the pictures directly from the magazine or printing them from the Internet, it is important to place them on the vision board and put it in a place where it will be easily observable. For example, it can be placed on a wall in front of one's computer. The key is to look at the vision board as frequently as possible (Earley, 2021). In this case, a person will have an opportunity to constantly envision their goals and not lose grip of them. At times, it happens that people understand that the goals they placed on the vision boards do not resonate with their inner selves anymore. Therefore, they should never be afraid to make changes, removing some of the visuals and attaching new ones.

Dr. Roberto Jimenez • *Manifest Your Best Life!*

Dr. Roberto Jimenez • *Manifest Your Best Life!*

Journaling: Future Scripting

Many people step on the pathway to success by using the power of writing. Similar to images, words help them identify their goals and focus on them more clearly. Journaling is one of the most effective ways of manifesting because it reinforces positive thinking about the future. One of the most common journaling techniques is represented by writing about one's goals in the present tense. This manifestation technique is called future scripting. It encourages people to write about the future as if they have already experienced it. For example, instead of writing, "I want to have/I will have a large house in 2025," it is crucial to write, "It's 2025 and I enjoy living in my large house." The main point of future scripting is to rewire the brain, making it believe that goals are reality. By writing about their dreams in the present tense, people make them look attainable. When these dreams are considered a part of existence, they are mentally transformed into a plan. Therefore, this approach to journaling helps people set new norms and feel that their ambitious goals will come to life. As a result, the pursuit of these goals will be less scary.

Gratitude is one of the most significant aspects of positive thinking. It encourages a person to accept everything that happens in their life. The power of gratitude is considerable because it helps overcome negativity and treat it with grace. Thus, keeping a gratitude journal is a crucial strategy that contributes to effective manifesting. By writing a list of things they are grateful for in their lives, people manage to stay focused on positivity. In the majority of cases, such lists contain things that brought them good emotions and made them happier at the particular moment. At the same time, it is crucial to remember that a gratitude list can also mention some difficulties and challenges people had to face in their lives. Indeed, these obstacles often encourage them to grow and become more mature. Therefore, it is also important to embrace these opportunities for development, reflecting on the key takeaways and insights from the times when things did not go smoothly. Accordingly, the main goal of a gratitude list is to help people remember that their life is full of good things. By writing and re-reading the compilation of these valuable memories, people will learn to focus on good aspects of their life even more. A gratitude list can motivate them to perceive more things with acceptance and love. This journaling technique usually encourages people to seek positivity every day.

By constantly expressing their gratitude, they will never lose their perspective of how valuable their experiences are. A gratitude list is something that can keep them motivated during the moments when they will face challenges in the future. Indeed, if people realize that difficulties they experienced in the past brought some useful lessons, benefitting them in the long-term perspective, they will build greater resilience when dealing with new issues. Overall, gratitude is

1
2
3
4
5
6
7
8
9
10
11
12
13
14
15
16
17
18
19
20
21
22
23
24
25

26	
27	
28	
29	
30	
31	
32	
33	
34	
35	
36	
37	
38	
39	
40	
41	
42	
43	
44	
45	
46	
47	
48	
49	
50	

Every individual can use the power of positive future-oriented thinking when writing a letter to self. This technique essentially contributes to deep self-reflection, which is one of the most significant foundations of effective manifesting. For instance, it is possible to create a letter to a future self. To use them as an instrument for manifesting goals and dreams, people have to define things they want to change in the future. When writing a letter, they should believe that their future selves have accomplished their goals and live happily. They might state something like, "Congratulations on starting your own company and becoming an entrepreneur of the year! I am so proud of you," or "I am so happy that you found a love of your life and started a family! You deserve to love and feel loved every day!" People can also mention how their future selves managed to deal with the challenges they are facing at the moment of writing a letter. The paper version of the letter should be placed in an envelope and then sealed. It is important to state the open date on the envelope. The letter should be stored in safe place where nobody could find it. One more option is to create an e-mail. For instance, it is possible to use an Internet service like FutureMe. In this case, a letter will be stored on a server and then sent on one's email automatically on a date that was previously picked by the user.

The benefits of this technique are considerable because such letters help people understand their current reality and desired future more clearly. Also, letters to future selves encourage them to identify the goals they want to attain most. It often happens that people forget about their plans. The process of writing motivates them to put everything on paper and make a promise to deliver these goals by certain deadline. Since these letters to future selves incorporate positive affirmations and the elements of future scripting, they encourage people to work towards their goals.

Writing letters from future selves to current selves is a slightly different approach to self-reflection. In this case, people have to imagine that they already live in the future, picturing that they have already attained their goals

by that moment. This technique encourages them to directly step into their better versions' shoes. For example, it is possible to write, "Do you know that I have started my own company, becoming an entrepreneur of the year? I know that you are so proud of me right now!" or "I am so happy to find a love of my life! I have just started a family and I have never felt more loved! This makes me feel great!" While a letter to one's future self is written from a perspective of a person, who still has not achieved these goals and only seeks to connect with their future successful life, a letter to one's current self puts the writer into the position of a leader, who has already implemented their plans. Many people, who aspire to manifest their goals, will find the experience of writing letters from future selves to current selves an emotionally rewarding experience.

Dr. Roberto Jimenez • *Manifest Your Best Life!*

While some people prefer focusing on short-term goals, it is always better to look at plans through a long-term perspective. This approach can help understand how the immediate attainment of short-term goals aligns with one's main purpose in life. Therefore, each individual should seek to write a 10-year plan, which will contain different goals and demonstrate how certain accomplishments will open the next phases of life, presenting new goals. The plan can take many forms ranging from a table or a diagram to a written list of goals that are placed into different categories. It is crucial to identify short-term, medium-term, and long-term goals. When choosing these goals, a person should always apply a SMART framework. It means that these goals have to be specific, measurable, attainable, relevant, and time-bound (Weintraub et al., 2021).

It is always important to start with the identification of one's key mission. For example, becoming a CEO of an organization that will distribute innovative technologies and contribute to sustainable development at the global scale is a mission that can qualify as a long-term goal. Therefore, it will be considered an ultimate goal that will inform the rest of the goals of smaller scale. Indeed, it will inspire a range of medium-term goals like getting 3 years of experience in a technological sector, launching a startup in the next 5 years, and using this time to build powerful business connections across all continents. Finally, short-term goals should represent some things that will take less time to accomplish. For example, a person might realize that to attain medium-term goals, it is important to enter a business college within the next year. Writing a 10-year plan is crucial because it encourages people to break down their large goals in life into smaller steps. Therefore, this element of manifesting helps them see their dreams as more achievable.

Specific

What am I going to do? Why is this important to me?

Measurable

How will I measure my success? How will I know when I have achieved my goal?

Attainable

What will I do to achieve this goal? How will I accomplish this goal?

Relevant

Is this goal worthwhile? How will achieving it help me? Does this goal fit my values?

Time-Bound

When will I accomplish my goal? How long will I give myself?

Action Plan

My goal is,

....

....

....

Date to finish	How will I measure my success?

Steps to Achieving my Goal

Description	Time Estimate	Completion date

Obstacles that may arise	How I will respond

Helpful Tools	Helpful Resources

Working Hard

While people should focus on positivity, they should never forget that their entire future is in their hands. **By acknowledging the influence of their own decisions, they have to recognize that they are in charge of their life. Accordingly, it means that every person should work hard to attain success because it rarely happens overnight (Zapata, 2022).** Even though support might come from unexpected sources, people should always count only on themselves when it comes to their personal development. Thus, they have to cultivate essential leadership skills. For example, every individual should remember that to attain success in certain career path, it is important to spend hundreds and even thousands of hours doing tasks that are relevant to this profession. When people are ready to work hard, they understand that it is crucial to own their mistakes and fix them. Therefore, this determination encourages them to accept challenges and convert them into opportunities for development. Manifesting per say will not bring considerable results if an individual constantly shifts the most important responsibilities to somebody else. **Indeed, working hard is what makes a person even more motivated to implement their goals and dreams.**

Color the Hard-Working Characteristics that apply to you:

Punctuality and dependability	Culturally fit
Initiative and flexibility	Team spirit
Motivation and priorities	Marketable
Learning and self-reliance	Detail-oriented
Stamina and perseverance	Leadership qualities

Manifesting is a process that promotes positive orientation in life. When humans have to work hard to implement some plans that will benefit their future, they have to invest in their motivation, which will drive their performance. Thus, they have to surround themselves with positive people, things, and events. **For instance, those who want to attain success should take a closer look at their friends, colleagues, and acquaintances, who spread negativity.** It is important to minimize contact with such individuals or stop communicating with them completely. Such people might even sabotage the development of others, directly interfering with this process. To enhance the success of manifesting, people have to make sure that their inner circle supports them.

It is also crucial to consume content that spreads positivity. Many people read inspirational books that promote positive beliefs. Others love watching films that show stories of success of the greatest leaders, who managed to change the world for the better. Some prefer exploring motivational TED talks, which share insights of researchers, who study the science of happiness and motivation.

When working towards ambitious goals and dreams, **people should also surround themselves with positive habits and events.** For example, it is important to cultivate feeling of joy by engaging in yoga, donating to organizations that help others, or volunteering (Zapata, 2022). These actions contribute to a sense of fulfillment, helping people experience more positive emotions. One of the best ways to seek support is to attend events that promote personal development. There are many training programs, mastermind group meetings, workshops, and seminars, which help participants grow new skills and learn from each other. By attending such events, people will boost their motivation and stay focused on their plan. This kind of environment often helps like-minded individuals find each other. Therefore, the given strategy serves as a meaningful source of emotional support, encouraging people who manifest their goals and dreams to stay confident, resilient, and motivated.

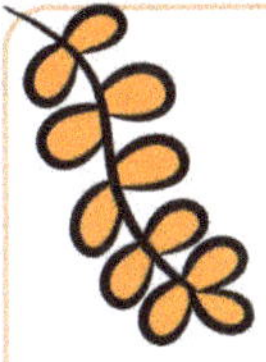

Surround Yourself with Greatness

Bye Bye to Negative Relationships

Welcome Positive & Good People

Get Outside Your Comfort Zone

Surround Yourself with People Who are Smart & Hardworking

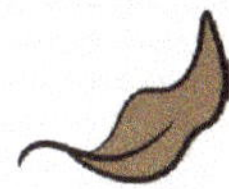

Conclusion

Overall, manifesting is a process that helps people transform their lives. It promotes the idea that if people genuinely believe in certain things, they will attract them. Harnessing the willpower and positive thinking, manifesting encourages people to set their goals clearly and start working toward them. By engaging in different practices like reciting positive affirmations, journaling, and creating vision boards, people can increase motivation and stay more focused. It is essential to remember that every person has inner resources to live the life of their dreams.

References

- **Davis, T. (2023). How to manifest something (manifest love, money, or anything).** https://www.berkeleywellbeing.com/how-to-manifest.html

- **Earley, B. (2021, March 24). Here's how to make a vision board for manifestation.** https://www.oprahdaily.com/life/a29959841/how-to-make-a-vision-board/

- **Raypole, C. (2020, September 1). Positive affirmations: Too good to be true?** https://www.healthline.com/health/mental-health/do-affirmations-work

- **Weintraub, J., Cassell, D., DePatie, T. (2021). Nursing flow through 'SMART' goal setting to decrease stress, increase engagement, and increase performance at work.** Journal of Occupational and Organizational Psychology, 94(2), 230-258. https://doi.org/10.1111/joop.12347

- **Zapata, K. (2022, July 23). How to manifest anything you desire.** https://www.oprahdaily.com/life/a30244004/how-to-manifest-anything/